W9-CND-309

Mysteries
OF LOST
CIVILIZATIONS

© Aladdin Books Ltd 1996

Designed and produced by
Aladdin Books Ltd
28 Percy Street
London W1P 0LD

First published in the United States in 1996 by
Copper Beech Books,
an imprint of
The Millbrook Press
2 Old New Milford Road
Brookfield,
Connecticut 06804

Editor: Katie Roden

Design: David West Children's Book Design

Designer: Flick Killerby

Picture Research: Brooks Krikler Research

Illustrators: Francis Phillipps;
Stephen Sweet – Simon Girling & Associates; Rob Shone

Printed in Belgium

Library of Congress Cataloging-in-Publication Data
Millard, Anne.
Lost civilizations / by Anne Millard : illustrated by Rob Shone... [et al.].
p. cm. -- (Mysteries of--)
Includes index.
Summary: Describes the cultures, cities, people, and objects of ancient civilizations
based on evidence from archaeological findings.
ISBN 0-7613-0534-3 (lib. bdg.)
1. Civilization, Ancient--History--Juvenile literature. 2. Extinct cities--History--
Juvenile literature. 3. Lost continents--History--Juvenile literature.
4. Archaeology--History--Juvenile literature. [1. Civilization, Ancient. 2. Cities
and towns, Ancient. 3. Archaeology.] I. Shone, Rob, ill. II. Title. III. Series.
CB311.M516 1996
930--dc20   96-20486 CIP AC

Mysteries
OF LOST
CIVILIZATIONS

Anne Millard

Copper Beech Books
Brookfield, Connecticut

6. Cadbury Fort
7. Stonehenge
8. Corsica
9. Carthage
10. Alexandria
11. Amarna
12. Abu Simbel
13. Meroe
14. Nubia
15. Great
    Zimbabwe
16. Crete
17. Thera
18. Olympia
19. Mycenae
20. Anatolia
21. Troy
22. Palmyra
23. Qumran

1. Rock Eagle Mound
2. Tenochtitlan
3. Lake Guatavita
4. Nazca Lines
5. Machu Picchu

24. Babylon
25. Edom
26. Dilmun
27. Bactria
28. Indus Valley
29. Altai tombs
30. Amazonian graves
31. Mount Li
32. Angkor
33. Easter Island

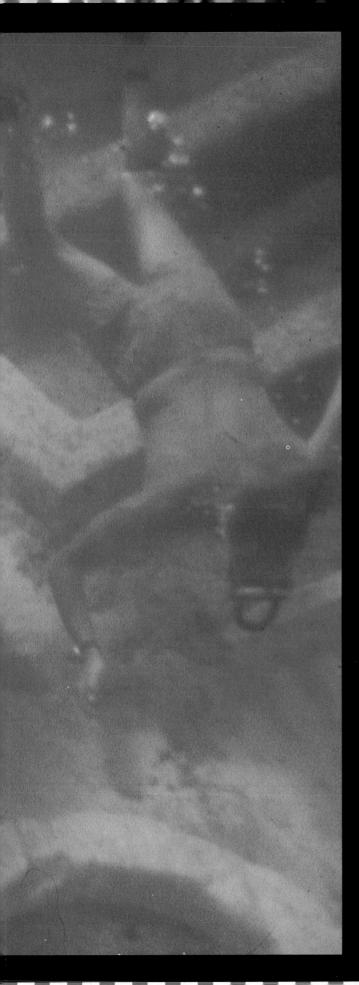

CONTENTS

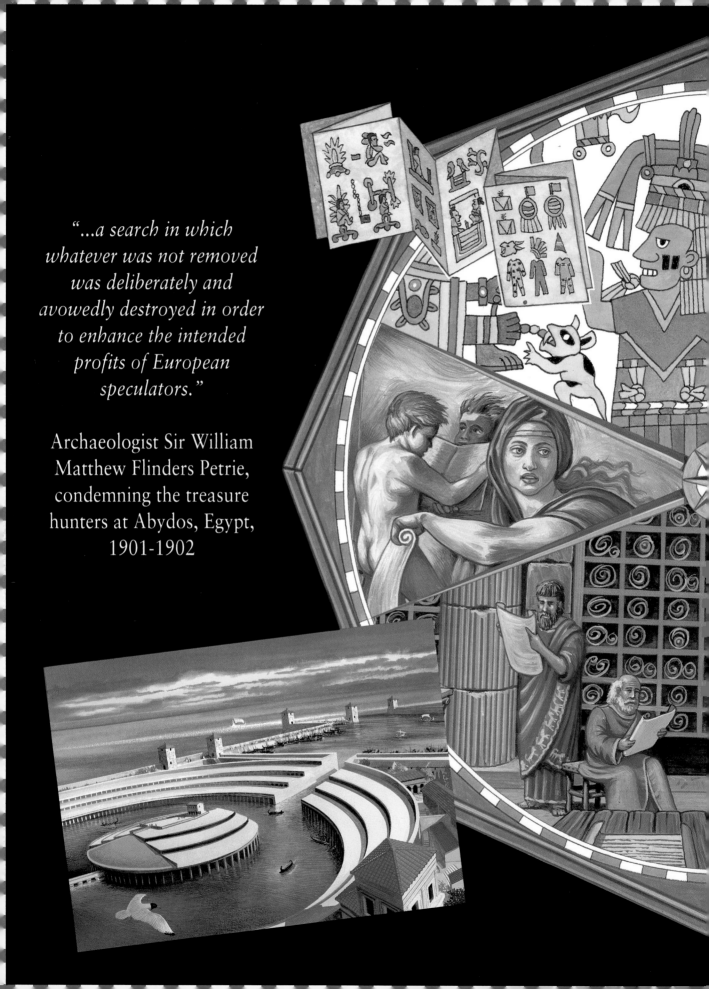

"...a search in which whatever was not removed was deliberately and avowedly destroyed in order to enhance the intended profits of European speculators."

Archaeologist Sir William Matthew Flinders Petrie, condemning the treasure hunters at Abydos, Egypt, 1901-1902

Introduction to THE MYSTERIES

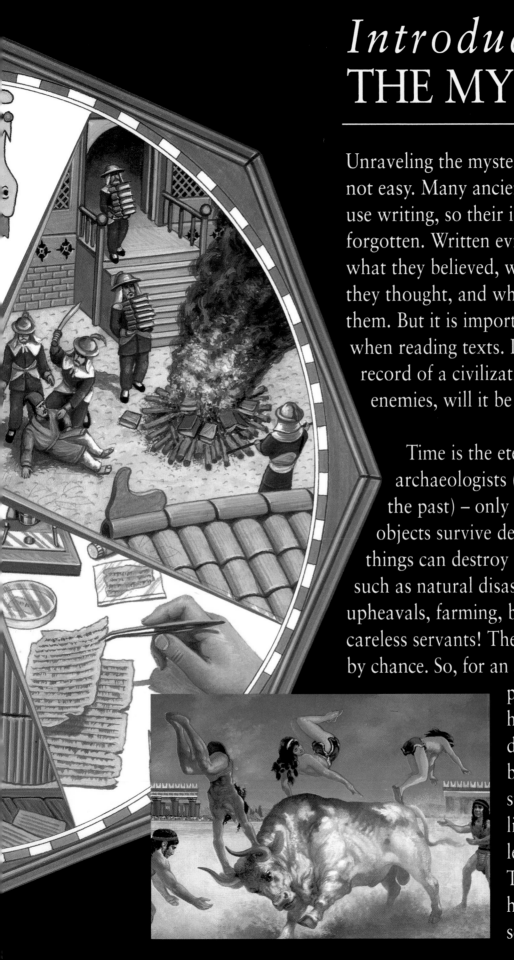

Unraveling the mysteries of the past is not easy. Many ancient peoples did not use writing, so their ideas and deeds are forgotten. Written evidence can tell us what they believed, what they did, what they thought, and what others thought of them. But it is important to be careful when reading texts. If the only surviving record of a civilization is written by its enemies, will it be a fair account?

Time is the eternal enemy of archaeologists (people who study the past) – only a few bodies and objects survive decay. Many other things can destroy clues to the past, such as natural disasters, wars, religious upheavals, farming, building – and even careless servants! They often survive only by chance. So, for an accurate view of the past, archeologists have to turn into detectives, examining buildings and objects, studying texts, and listening to what legends tell them. They also need the help of all the latest scientific techniques.

Hidden PLACES

Some places are destroyed and disappear, almost without trace, until an archaeologist tracks down their remains. Sometimes a place is mentioned only in a much later text and is dismissed as a legend.

A good example is the siege of Troy (in modern-day Turkey), by the ancient Greeks. For centuries, the *Iliad* (700s B.C.), Homer's poem about the Trojan war, was regarded as fantasy. But an amateur archaeologist called Heinrich Schliemann passionately believed that it was true. In 1870, he began digging in the area where Homer had placed Troy – and found it! Excavations have proved that Homer knew many details about a civilization that had vanished centuries before he was born. Stories and songs had kept alive memories of such details as the city's defenses and the soldiers' armor. We cannot yet prove that the beautiful Helen of Troy existed, or what the wooden horse was (left), but we have learned not to simply dismiss the legends of the past.

"Was this the face that launch'd a thousand ships
And burnt the topless towers of Ilium?"
Description of Helen of Troy in Christopher Marlowe's play *Doctor Faustus*, c. 1588

Lost and FOUND

Many buildings referred to in ancient writings are now totally destroyed, such as the Roman emperor Nero's fabulous Golden House. Sometimes we find ruins that can be identified beyond doubt, like Pompeii in Italy, which was buried by a volcanic eruption. But even if archaeologists can identify a site and have ancient texts describing it, they still have difficulty imagining what it was like at its peak. Ancient Greek writers said that the burial complex of King Amenemhet III of Egypt was one of the most magnificent buildings they had ever seen; now, only dreary piles of mud bricks are left! Only if we have a picture of such a place can we begin to imagine it in all its glory.

Can destruction ever have benefits? Sometimes it can reveal other treasures. During World War II, a bomb destroyed the ancient church of St. Bride's in London, England. This tragedy gave archaeologists a chance to excavate the site. They found earlier churches going back about 1,400 years and a Roman pavement from the second century A.D. St. Bride's was then rebuilt.

ROUND TABLE RIDDLES

In medieval legend, Camelot was the headquarters of King Arthur. If it existed, it was nothing like the fairy tale castles of Hollywood films! It may have been an old Celtic hill-fort, reoccupied by the English war-leader – a place of earth ramparts and wooden battlements. Archaeologists have found such a site at Cadbury Fort in England, which some people think might be Camelot.

GARDENS OF LEGEND

The Hanging Gardens of Babylon were built for a queen from the hill country, who was homesick for the plains of Babylonia. They were so completely destroyed that we cannot even identify the foundations. However there are many theories on what they looked like!

ON THE TRAIL OF KING MINOS

In 1893, the archaeologist Sir Arthur Evans was shown some seal-stones covered in strange pictures. He tracked them to Crete, the legendary home of King Minos. Evans began to dig, and unearthed the mighty Minoan civilization. It had been ruined and forgotten – except in legend.

THE LIGHT OF THE MEDITERRANEAN

Built in about 280 B.C., the lighthouse of Alexandria, in Egypt, was 390 feet (117 m) high. Its beam could be seen for 30 miles (50 km). It was toppled by an earthquake in the 1300s, but we still have accounts and pictures of it. Pieces of it have been found in the harbor.

An Indian mystery

Excavations by Sir Robert Eric Mortimer Wheeler (1890-1976) revealed artifacts (below), seal-stones (left), and buildings of the Indus Valley civilization of ancient India. They invented their own writing system, but no one has managed to decipher it yet. Will we ever know who their rulers were, the purpose of their great ceremonial bath, or the identity of their god, the Lord of the Animals?

A GREAT TRIBUTE

In the fifth century B.C., the Greek sculptor Phidias made a great statue of the god Zeus to go in his temple at Olympia. It was 43 feet (13 m) tall and made of gold and ivory. In A.D. 393, a Roman emperor took it to Constantinople, but a fire swept the place where it was kept in A.D. 462, destroying it completely.

THE EFFECTS OF WAR

Conquerors often try to wipe out all traces of their enemies' culture. This was the fate of the Aztec and Inca peoples at the hands of 16th-century Spanish explorers. The great Aztec capital of Tenochtitlan was demolished. Its remains still lie under modern Mexico City.

The Stuff of LEGENDS

When something really exciting happens, people like to tell the story over and over again. Unless it is written down immediately, it changes as time passes. Details get left out; others are added; the deeds of two or more people can be credited to one "super-hero." Over time, people even forget what some things were or what they meant, so they invent explanations – which are often wrong! A story might be given a new meaning so that it fits in with the politics and religion of the time. But somewhere, buried in every story, there remains a kernel of truth.

THE ULTIMATE QUEST
People have searched all over the world for Atlantis (see page 13), but many now believe that the story was inspired by Minoan Crete (see page 11). The memory of the great island kingdom with its powerful navy, the importance of bulls in its religion, and its sudden decline had become mixed up with natural disasters and myths. The stories were muddled and misunderstood as time passed, but some accounts do seem to contain an echo of the great Minoan civilization.

CONQUISTADORES!
The early Spanish conquerors of America were driven by a desire to serve God (by converting people to Christianity) and their king (by winning him an empire). But they were also ruthless and greedy, out to make their own fortunes from the gold and silver of the "New World." In Colombia, they heard the fantastic but true story of El Dorado – the "Gilded Man" (see page 13).

Lake Guatavita
(Colombia)

THE GOLDEN RULER

When a king came to the throne in the region of Lake Guatavita, Colombia, he was covered in gold dust then sailed to the middle of the lake, where he threw in gold offerings to the gods. Imagination and greed embroidered the story, and tales spread, of a city and a land made of gold. For two centuries, people searched for "El Dorado" and it cost many lives. Others tried to drain the lake, but failed.

ERUPTION AND DEVASTATION

Thera (now Santorini), 72 miles (120 km) north of Crete, was an outpost of Minoan culture. In about 1450 B.C., there was a huge volcanic eruption which blew away most of the island. It also caused a tidal wave that wrecked Minoan settlements in northern Crete.

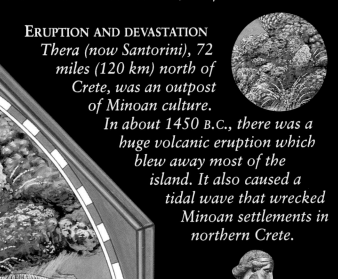

THE STUFF OF LEGENDS

The Greek writer Plato (above) wrote about Atlantis, a lost island kingdom which sank below the waves in a terrible disaster. Debates have raged ever since. Did Plato invent it? Was it based on Thera and Crete? Or was it another lost place? The tale had been passed on by word of mouth for almost 200 years before Plato heard it – plenty of time for errors to creep in!

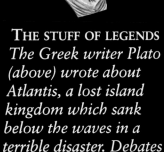

Thera (Santorini)

King Solomon's mines

Some people have embarked on quests for things mentioned in the Bible – the Ark of the Covenant, the treasure from the temple of Jerusalem, Noah's Ark, and many others. Others have looked for places. The fabulous mines of King Solomon caught people's imagination and inspired films and novels. When the ruins of Great Zimbabwe (below) were found in Africa, some suggested that these were the famous mines. But Zimbabwe belongs to a much later African empire. Solomon's mines remain out of our grasp.

Can texts really lead us to lost places? Ancient Mesopotamian texts refer to a place called Dilmun, describing it as so wonderful that, until recently, scholars dismissed it as fantasy. Studies of earlier texts and ruins have shown that it was a staging post in the trade between Sumer and the Indus Valley. When the trade ceased, Dilmun was forgotten – in fact, it was the island of Bahrain!

The Lost CULTURES

All cultures change over time. We can follow the developments of long-lived civilizations, like those of ancient Egypt and China, over thousands of years. We can see how life has evolved in Europe since the fall of the Roman Empire in A.D. 476. People's ways of life have changed, but we can trace elements from the past to the present.

Even if a culture seems to have been wiped out, some things survive and are absorbed by a new civilization. Memories of lost cultures may live on in texts or in legends. Then one day, archaeologists may find solid remains. Archaeologists often discover many surprises while exploring lost cultures. Some people still find it hard to accept that young Minoans (left) would leap through the horns of charging bulls – yet there are pictures and statues to prove it. Did they risk their lives in this way to please a god? Perhaps they believed that this god tossed their land with earthquakes as the bull tossed the athletes with its horns.

> "…[the archaeologist] brings to light a mass of objects illustrating the arts and handicrafts of the past, the temples in which men worshiped, the houses in which they lived, the setting in which their lives were spent."
>
> Sir Leonard Woolley, *Digging up the Past*, 1930

Decline, Destruction, AND DEATH

Some flourishing cultures have been quickly and totally destroyed, but this rarely happens so dramatically. Usually, many factors combine and there is a long, slow decline to extinction. Years of bad weather may cause famine, farmland can lose its fertility if over-used, and wood supplies run out if people cut down trees without replanting them. A vital river may change course or a harbor may silt up. Earthquakes, floods, and other natural disasters may occur. Trade may be disrupted or there may be wars and invasions. The people of a declining society may simply emigrate or decide to adopt the ways of more successful neighbors.

How do cultures become legends? Through distortions of fact that happen over time. For example, one group of the Sea Peoples (see page 17) was called the Peleset. After their defeat by Egypt, they retreated and the land where they settled was named after them – Palestine. They appear in the Bible as the Philistines, the archenemies of the Hebrews.

OMENS OF DISASTER
A fiery comet in the early 1500s terrified the Aztecs of Central America. Was this a sign that their gods were angry with them? For ten years, many strange events occurred. The Aztecs thought they were doomed; they were – the Spaniards arrived (see page 12).

THE INCAS' LAST STAND
In 1911, the explorer Hiram Bingham set out for the Andes, armed with texts telling of cities where the last Incas had fought off the Spaniards. He found Machu Picchu, an Inca city that for 300 years had been hidden by the jungle.

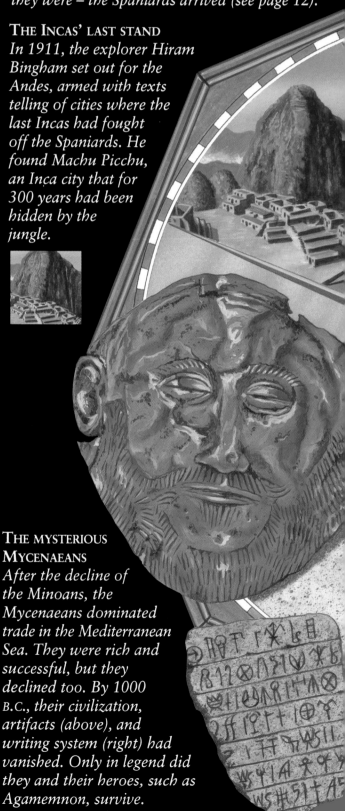

THE MYSTERIOUS MYCENAEANS
After the decline of the Minoans, the Mycenaeans dominated trade in the Mediterranean Sea. They were rich and successful, but they declined too. By 1000 B.C., their civilization, artifacts (above), and writing system (right) had vanished. Only in legend did they and their heroes, such as Agamemnon, survive.

MYTHS OF THE MAYA
The Maya were once seen as a peace-loving people. But archeologists have begun to decode their writing and it is clear that rival city-states fought constantly for power. Overfarming contributed to their decline, but so did these wars.

An advanced culture
The state of Meroe flourished from about 50 B.C. until about A.D. 350 and traded with Egypt, Africa, Greece, Rome, and India. Its culture was a blend of local customs and those of Egypt and other countries (such as pyramid tombs for its kings, below). Meroe's farmers grew cotton, brought from India. Its metalsmiths worked iron, and their methods spread into Africa. One text claims Meroe was so rich that its prisoners were held in golden chains! Attacks by other peoples led to its decline, but it collapsed after an invasion by the King of Axum in East Africa.

EGYPT
River Nile
Meroe
NUBIA

ATEN'S CITY
One king of Egypt, Akhenaton, believed that Aten was the only god. He built a new capital at Tel el Amarna and banned worship of other gods. But after his death, Amarna was left to the mercy of the desert sands.

INVADERS FROM THE SEA
Ancient Egyptian texts describe invasions by mysterious "Sea Peoples." These were from the declining Mycenaean empire, looking for new homes. In about 1190 B.C., they invaded what is now Turkey, wiping out the Hittites (see page 18). They were finally defeated by Rameses III of Egypt, and scattered all over the Mediterranean.

Who Were THEY?

One clue to a people's identity is their language. One ancient language was Proto-Indo-European. Over the centuries, the groups who spoke it began to drift apart. They traveled across Europe and into the Middle East, then on to India and Turkestan. Each group changed its language so much that they would not have been able to communicate if they had met. The family of languages now called Indo-European includes almost all European languages, Russian, Ukranian, Armenian, Iranian, and most of the major languages of India and Pakistan, as well as many ancient languages.

THE KEY TO A LOST PEOPLE
In the 1970s, strange items (left) appeared on the antiques market. Scholars investigated them and tracked down a whole new culture, which had flourished in Bactria in 2500-1500 B.C. The Bactrians were wealthy traders who controlled the land route between the Indus Valley and Mesopotamia.

HITTITE CONQUESTS
By 2000 B.C., the Hittites had arrived in Anatolia from north of the Black Sea. They gradually established an empire and a writing system (below). At first they were Egypt's enemies, but then they sealed a treaty. They were wiped out by the Sea Peoples (see page 17).

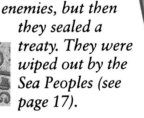

Brutal invaders... or peaceful settlers?
Because their victims wrote all the known records of their actions, the Vikings have been regarded as pirates for centuries. Some were, but most were farmers and skilled craftspeople. Others were daring merchants who traveled as far as the Middle East. There were also intrepid explorers who founded colonies in Russia, Iceland, Greenland, and North America.

THE FIRST MINOANS

In about 6000 B.C., the ancestors of the Minoans arrived on the island of Crete, probably from Anatolia. Archeologists have traced their progress from simple farmers to a great trading nation. They invented their own writing system, which we call Linear A, but as yet no one can read it. Linear B, the writing of the later Mycenaeans (see page 16), is readable because it was an early form of Greek, which is an Indo-European language.

THE ROSE-RED CITY

In the fourth century B.C., an Arab tribe, the Nabataeans, set up a kingdom in what had been Edom. They controlled the trade routes from Arabia and the Red Sea to the Mediterranean, and became rich and powerful. Their great capital, Petra, was built of a pinkish stone and surrounded by cliffs. Its entrance was a narrow cleft in the rocks, while its temples and tombs were cut into the cliffs. It came under Roman rule in A.D. 106, and gradually declined.

THE MISSING MARVELS OF ANGKOR

The Khmers of Cambodia expanded their empire after A.D. 800 and built a great temple complex at Angkor Wat and a capital at Angkor Thom. But the Thais defeated them in the early 1400s and their buildings were lost in the jungle. They were found by chance, by Henri Mouhot in 1860.

What is the oldest alphabet?
The earliest writing systems used hieroglyphs (pictures) rather than letters. The Phoenician system was then adapted by the ancient Greeks into the first alphabet. The letter O is thought to be the most ancient written letter. We know it was used as early as 1300 B.C. – and it has not changed its shape since.

"Moreover, all this ruin was brought upon the Romans by a woman, a fact which in itself caused them the greatest shame."

Cassius Dio of Rome, writing over 100 years after Boudicca's revolt

Missing PEOPLE

A society may record the deeds of its great men and women, but over time the texts can be lost or destroyed. Our knowledge about them is therefore limited, but there is always hope that an excavation will find more texts!

If the few accounts of an event are written by one side only, they are likely to be biased. The English revolt of A.D. 60-61, led by Queen Boudicca of the Iceni tribe, is a good example. It killed thousands of Roman colonists and soldiers, important towns were destroyed and Rome nearly lost its new land. But the Romans won in the end and wrote of a struggle of law, order, and civilization against savagery and ignorance. Boudicca and the English who died were portrayed as fierce and unworthy. If the Iceni had kept records, they might have written of their heroic struggle to drive out invaders whose greed, cruelty, and brutal treatment of Queen Boudicca had made them unworthy of being treated with honor or mercy.

The Forgotten WOMEN

Our knowledge about women in history is limited. This is partly due to destruction of records over time, and partly because some societies were ruled by men who believed women were of little importance and so denied them any rights or power outside the home. The records of such a culture give few details about women. If a male-dominated society was threatened by a woman, its writers usually did their best to blacken her name. We can find many "lost" women through texts and excavations, but we must be very careful not to be fooled by the attitudes of the authors of the texts!

How did Queen Boudicca die?
After her defeat, in A.D. 61, Boudicca committed suicide rather than be taken prisoner by the Romans. Records say that the Iceni gave her a costly burial, but it is not clear where. Several places in England claim the honor of being the site of the queen's last resting place. One theory says that she lies under Platform 8 of London's King's Cross railroad station! Will this mystery ever be solved?

A KING WITH A DIFFERENCE
Women were honored in ancient Egypt but only a man could ascend to the throne. A few women got around this rule. Queen Hatshepsut claimed that the god Amun had chosen her to rule and reigned as "King." After her death, her nephew destroyed her monuments to remove all traces of her. Archaeologists are now defeating him by putting the pieces back together again!

PAYING THE PRICE
Zenobia, Queen of Palmyra, in Syria, carved her own empire by conquering Rome's eastern provinces. When she was finally defeated, the Romans tried to humiliate her by making her walk in the emperor's victory parade – but she had the last laugh. She married a senator and became a famous hostess!

22

THE MYSTERIOUS QUEEN

Nefertiti was the wife of Akhenaton (see page 17). After their deaths, their enemies tried to destroy all records of their religious revolution, leaving us with many questions. Did Nefertiti support her husband's worship of Aten? Did she become "King" for a while? When and how did she die?

THE MOST FAMOUS QUEEN IN HISTORY

Our information about Queen Cleopatra VII comes mainly from Roman records. She had scared the Romans by helping Mark Antony to fight against Octavian (later Emperor Augustus). She was a good ruler, but the Roman writers described her as unworthy.

THE LEGEND OF SHEBA

The Bible tells how the Queen of Sheba learned of the wisdom of King Solomon and went to visit him. In fact, Sheba's kingdom was rich from trade. She and Solomon were probably making a trade deal!

BURIED IN STATE

Wonderfully preserved in an intricate tomb, surrounded by treasures and wrapped in beautiful silks, a mysterious Chinese noblewoman was discovered by archaeologists in the 1980s. Modern medical techniques have shown the illnesses she suffered from and how she passed her last hours.w

A scandal in Rome

Legend says that a young woman once disguised herself as a man and was elected Pope (the head of the Catholic Church)! She was nicknamed "Pope Joan." The story may have arisen because in the tenth century A.D. there were some very weak Popes. A mother and daughter called Theodora and Marozia gained influence over several of them, even deciding who the new Popes should be!

People of LEGEND

Every country and culture has its legends. It is tempting to quote a legend to help prove a theory about a piece of history, but we must use legends with great care. A legend may be based on real events but it is not always clear which parts are true, which are based on fact but have been changed, and which are later additions. It can be exciting if, while studying a text or excavating a site, archaeologists find something that fits in with, or explains, a legend; but they do not normally set out to prove that a legend is true.

THE BEAST IN THE LABYRINTH
Legend says the Minotaur was half bull, half man. He lived in the Labyrinth (maze) at Knossos and ate human flesh. How did the story begin? Did people later misinterpret tales of bull-leaping? Perhaps the kings of Knossos wore bull masks for religious rites and this inspired the legend.

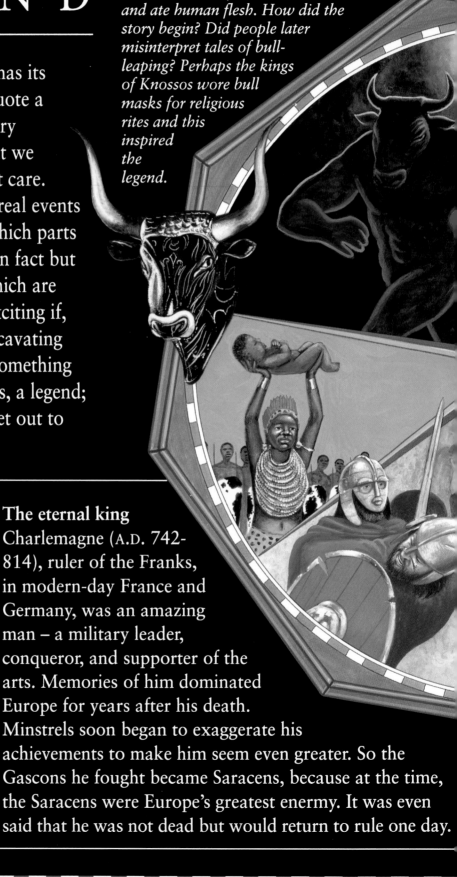

The eternal king
Charlemagne (A.D. 742-814), ruler of the Franks, in modern-day France and Germany, was an amazing man – a military leader, conqueror, and supporter of the arts. Memories of him dominated Europe for years after his death. Minstrels soon began to exaggerate his achievements to make him seem even greater. So the Gascons he fought became Saracens, because at the time, the Saracens were Europe's greatest enemy. It was even said that he was not dead but would return to rule one day.

RIDING THROUGH THE GLEN

England's best-loved folk hero is Robin Hood... but who was he? Over the centuries, writers have altered his identity to suit the views of the time – from a peasant to an earl!

Was Robin Hood one man, or did the deeds of several outlaws get credited to one person? Legend places Robin in the reign of King Richard I (1189-1199), but an outlaw called Robin Hood is recorded as living later. Did he use the name of the earlier outlaw, or was he the real one?

A TERRIBLE SACRIFICE

When civil war raged in 18th-century West Africa, legend says that Queen Pokou and her people fled, but reached a vast, swiftly-flowing river. In return for a safe crossing, the gods demanded the sacrifice of a child. Pokou could have killed a poor woman's child, but she sacrificed her own son.

Do legend and reality ever get mixed up? Myth and fact often become confused as a story is passed down through the centuries. For example, legend says that an early Count of Anjou, in France, met a beautiful girl called Melusine in a forest. He fell in love, married her and they lived happily – until he found out that she was the daughter of the Devil! Melusine's descendants are said to include England's Plantagenet kings (1154-1399), the ancestors of today's British royal family.

WARRIOR WOMEN

Greek writers told about Mycenaean heroes who fought the Amazons, a tribe of women, who went to what is now Russia. Scholars dismissed the stories, but in the 1950s archaeologists found the graves of a nomadic tribe in Russia. Some women's graves contained weapons and armor of the right date for the Amazons.

ROUND TABLE RIDDLES

Who was the real King Arthur? Early texts suggest he was a Roman Briton who fought the Saxons. Details like the sword Excalibur, his knights, and the Round Table came later. When the Saxons won, some Britons fled to Wales, where bards reworked the story. Medieval minstrels, 15th-century poets, and Victorian writers added to it, creating the legend as it is today.

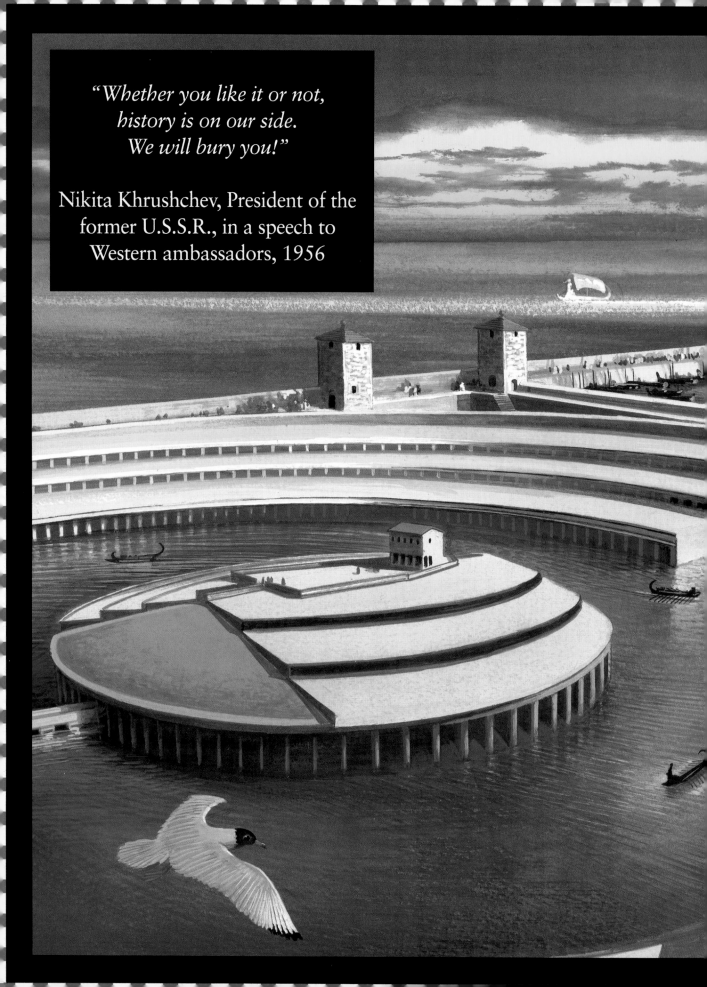

"*Whether you like it or not, history is on our side. We will bury you!*"

Nikita Khrushchev, President of the former U.S.S.R., in a speech to Western ambassadors, 1956

Mysterious OBJECTS

Considering the destruction caused by time, nature, and people, an amazing number of buildings, texts, and objects have survived! But these represent only a tiny fraction of the glories of past civilizations. A site can be destroyed and completely lost if we have no references to it in any texts.

Texts mention many places, but we do not know where they were. Some are found by careful investigation. Sometimes we know where a city was but it is difficult to get at – the ruins of Pompeii, for example. The Romans destroyed the city of Carthage, in North Africa, but thanks to careful excavation archaeologists are finding out about Rome's great rival and know what its magnificent harbor (left) and splendid docks were like.

Some people just cannot resist a challenge! They continue to search for objects and places that most scholars believe no longer exist, such as biblical objects like Noah's Ark and the Ark of the Covenant.

The Lost
B O O K S

It is bad enough when books and the vital information they hold are destroyed by accident. It is awful if they are tampered with to fit the ideas of the day. But history is littered with instances of the deliberate destruction of books. Many rulers have destroyed texts to erase the memory of enemies or burned books to stop the spread of "unacceptable" ideas.

One of the greatest thrills for an archaeologist is to find a text with vital historical information. Such a find was the Turin Papyrus, which gave a full list of Egypt's kings. The papyrus was so badly damaged during transport that experts are still trying to piece it back together again.

THE LOSS OF A LONG HISTORY
The Maya and Aztecs made scrolls of bark or deerskin with pictures of their past. The Spaniards burned most of them and had a new one, the Codex Mendoza, *made for their king, showing Aztec daily life.*

MISSING RECORDS
The Library of Alexandria held about 500,000 books and scholars came from far and wide to read them. Part of it was burned down during Caesar's campaign in Egypt (48 B.C.). The rest was destroyed in the A.D. 270s. Think of all the historical information we have lost!

Have ancient writings influenced our lives? We owe a lot to the wisdom of the past, which has come to us via the Greeks and Romans. The Egyptians invented the 365-day calendar and divided the day into 24 hours. The Babylonians used a system of numbers based on 60, from which we get 360 degrees in a circle, 60 minutes in an hour, and 60 seconds in a minute.

FATAL OPINIONS

In 221 B.C., Cheng, the ruler of Qin province, became the emperor of all China. When he heard that some scholars were criticizing him, he ordered the burning of all books, old and new, that might be used against him. Later he had 460 scholars executed.

The Dead Sea scrolls

In 1947, a shepherd boy found a cave at Qumran, on the shores of the Dead Sea. It contained some strange, ancient scrolls. Over the next few years, other caves and scrolls were discovered. The study of these texts was held up by scholarly, political, and religious rivalry, but they are now becoming available. The scrolls contain biblical texts, writings about the Bible, calendars, and hymns. They date from the first centuries B.C. and A.D. and were probably hidden during the Jewish revolts of A.D. 66 and 132, to save them from the Romans. They tell us about religious life before the birth of Christ and so are important to Christians, Jews, and Muslims alike.

THE SECRET GOSPELS

In the early days of Christianity, there were many different Christian groups. The Gnostics claimed to have secret knowledge, so the Church had their writings destroyed. One Gnostic buried his books at Nag Hammadi in Egypt. They were found by a farmer a few years ago!

WORDS OF WISDOM

A Sibyl was a Roman prophetess (a woman who could foresee the future). One Sibyl sold three books of her writings to King Tarquinius of Rome. The Sibylline prophecies were said to be very accurate and were consulted in times of trouble. They were destroyed by fire in 83 B.C., so we will never know how accurate they were.

Why Were They M A D E ?

People in the past were prepared to go to great lengths to make and build things, using up vast amounts of time and energy (when lives were much shorter than today). What made Stone Age hunters, who needed all their energy to survive in an Ice Age, go deep into caves to produce wonders like the Lascaux paintings (see page 32)? It is often difficult to work out how and why things were made. For example, some people still find it hard to believe that so much effort went into building Egypt's pyramids simply for them to be used as tombs. When we have no texts, just objects or ruins, it is even more difficult to interpret them.

Were old towns like modern ones?
In the town of Çatal Hüyük (in what is now Turkey), one of the first towns in the world, there were no roads and the houses were entered through a hole in the roof! The town had wide trading links and was very rich. Its citizens may have feared that jealous neighbors might try to attack them.

THE STANDING STONES

The peoples of Bronze Age Europe (3500-1000 B.C.) have left behind many monuments made of menhirs (upright stones). Some are in long lines; others are in circles. The most famous circle is Stonehenge (left) in southern England. Clearly it was built for religious rites, perhaps related to the Sun, as it faces the midsummer rising and midwinter setting of the Sun. But what about the stones with human faces on the island of Corsica (top)? Do they represent gods, heroes, or enemies?

AN EVERLASTING MEMORIAL

Native Americans built the Rock Eagle Effigy Mound in A.D. 500. Its wingspan is 120 ft (36 m). This is one of many monuments left by cultures that flourished from 1000 B.C. to A.D. 1500 in the Ohio and Mississippi river valleys.

Many built mounds. Some were for burials or had palaces on top. Others must have had religious use, but without written evidence we can only guess at it.

MYSTERIOUS MONUMENTS

Easter Island is only 15.5 miles (26 km) long, yet between A.D. 600 and 1500, its Polynesian people carved about 1,000 huge stone heads. Were they to honor great ancestors? Civil war and famine meant that statue building ceased.

PICTURES IN THE SAND

The Nazca people flourished along the south coast of Peru from about 200 B.C. to A.D. 600. They made lines across the desert by clearing away the stones and exposing the sand. Some of the lines are several miles long, some form patterns, and others depict huge monkeys, spiders, and birds. Were they drawn to please gods in the sky?

Guardians of the dead

Models of servants were placed in the graves of early Chinese kings and nobles, but the First Emperor (221-210 B.C.) outdid them all! In his tomb at Mount Li, a whole army, sculpted in terracotta, was buried. Over 8,000 life-sized models have been found so far. Most are foot soldiers, but there are also horses, chariots, and officers. Three attempts had been made on Cheng's life. He must have wanted a safe afterlife, guarded by his most trusted warriors.

LAWS OF STONE

King Asoka of India (272-231 B.C.) set up this pillar (right) to mark the spot where the Buddha first taught. Writings on many other pillars across India told of Asoka's laws to encourage peace and happiness in his land.

THE FIRST EGYPTIAN DAM

Recent excavations in Egypt have found that, in about 2600 B.C., the Egyptians were building a dam to protect villages from floods rushing down a narrow valley. But a flood destroyed the dam before it was completed.

"*Treasure hunting is as old as Man; scientific archaeology is a modern development, but in its short life... it has done marvels.*"

Sir Leonard Woolley, *Digging up the Past*, 1940

New Ideas and
INVESTIGATIONS

Archaeologists are leading the battle to find the lost treasures of the past. Their excavations are still uncovering hidden objects, buildings, texts, cities, and even entire civilizations. Historians and language experts then analyze the material. Unlike the archaeologists of the past, today's researchers are able to call upon specialized scientists and the latest modern technology to help them.

Archaeology is now more popular than ever before. Books and TV programs have made it exciting, and air travel means that thousands of people can now visit the world's wonders. This is great for tourism, but it can also cause archaeological problems. Too many people walking over sites can destroy the very things they have come to see! The caves at Lascaux, France, have been closed since 1963. While they were open to visitors, algae had entered the caves. It spread rapidly and began to destroy the 17,000-year-old paintings (left).

Faces from THE PAST

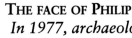

THE FACE OF PHILIP
In 1977, archaeologists found what they believed was the tomb of the Macedonian king Philip II, but they had no proof. An expert built up a clay face over the skull found in the tomb. It belonged to a man aged 40-50, with a scar over his right eye. We know Philip was wounded (and probably blinded) by an arrow in his eye – so it must be his tomb.

All historians dream about how wonderful it would be to meet people from the past, and, very occasionally, this dream almost comes true. Ancient Egyptians mummified their dead, so we have the thrill of looking at the faces of some of the pharaohs and their subjects. Sometimes natural conditions have preserved ancient bodies and faces in an excellent condition. Archaeologists can also turn to the modern police technique of rebuilding a face over the bones of a skull. Experts use clay to build up the muscles, tissues, and features such as the nose and mouth, until an ancient face looks out at them once again.

The Ice Man

One autumn day, about 5,000 years ago, a man was trudging through the Alps of Austria when he was caught in a blizzard. He lay down to sleep, and never awoke. His body, preserved by the ice, was found in 1991. We are getting valuable information about life in his time from his possessions. But why was he all alone? Was he a trader, a shepherd, or a priest? Had he left his village in a hurry?

BURIED IN THE BOG

The bogs of northern Europe have preserved many bodies, slain and thrown into the mud. We know that Iron Age people often made human sacrifices to their gods and goddesses. Were these bodies sacrificial victims? Some may have been criminals being punished or volunteers who hoped to bring luck to their tribe by pleasing the gods.

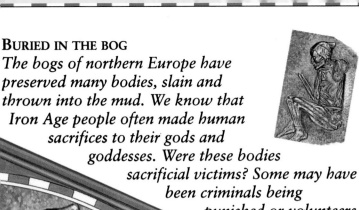

VICTIMS OF VESUVIUS

In A.D. 79, Mount Vesuvius in Italy erupted and the city of Pompeii was buried by ash and pumice stone. Most of its inhabitants fled, but those who stayed were suffocated by fumes. Their bodies decayed, but the ash hardened around them, preserving their impressions. By filling the hollows with plaster, archeologists can make replicas of the ancient bodies.

A GAZE FROM THE PAST

She lived in ancient Egypt and was about 14 when she died. Her mummy was reduced to bones. She suffered from a nose complaint and had lost both legs from the knee down, but we do not know if this happened before or after her death. This mysterious girl's face has been rebuilt on her skull and even given makeup.

THE FACE OF A KING

Timur Leng (Timur the Lame, 1336-1405), known in the West as Tamerlane, carved an empire in the Middle East and Central Asia. When historians opened his tomb, they asked experts to build up the face over the skull they found. It revealed the strong character of the ruthless warlord!

A GRAND SEND-OFF

Because their graves were cut into ground that was permanently frozen, the burials of nomadic chieftains and their families have been well preserved in the Altai Mountains of Kazakhstan. Objects of wood, cloth, and leather, sacrificed horses, and tattooed bodies have all survived since 400-200 B.C.

What can modern medicine tell us about people of the past?
Medical knowledge can help historians greatly. Most statues of Alexander the Great show him with his chin in the air and his head to one side. People thought it showed his arrogance. Recently, two doctors have suggested that he may have had a rare eye disease called Brown's Syndrome. The only way for sufferers to see properly is to hold their head in the way shown in the statues.

Methods of the FUTURE

Science, technology, medicine – all have made rapid progress over the last few years, greatly helping scholars and archaeologists. There are new techniques to help them find things and others to help them date those that they find. They can reconstruct an ancient landscape by finding and analyzing pollen and tiny organisms from a site. Medical techniques can now reveal more about ancient bodies and analyze blood and DNA. Science can help to conserve things better than ever and to detect fakes, too – forgers, beware!

Do people ever fake ancient finds?
The skull of "Piltdown Man," found in 1912, was hailed as a "missing link" in evolution. In 1953, it was proved to be a fake. An old trunk was found that belonged to a curator at the Natural History Museum, in London, England, at the time. It is stained with the same chemicals as those used by the hoaxer!

THE PRIDE OF THE FLEET
The Mary Rose *sank in 1545 near Plymouth, England. She settled on the seabed, where silt preserved one half. Raised in 1982, she is providing valuable details about Tudor life and ship building.*

WHAT LIES BELOW?
Opening and examining tombs takes time and money. Archaeologists use special equipment to detect underground hollows in some areas. If a tomb is found, a hole is drilled and a camera put in. Photos are taken to see if it is worth opening.

VIRTUAL HISTORY
Have you ever looked at ruins and wondered what the original building was like? Thanks to computers, you can now find out. Plans of a ruin can be used to produce a 3-D reconstruction. You can see the building as its original occupants knew it.

AERIAL ARCHAEOLOGY

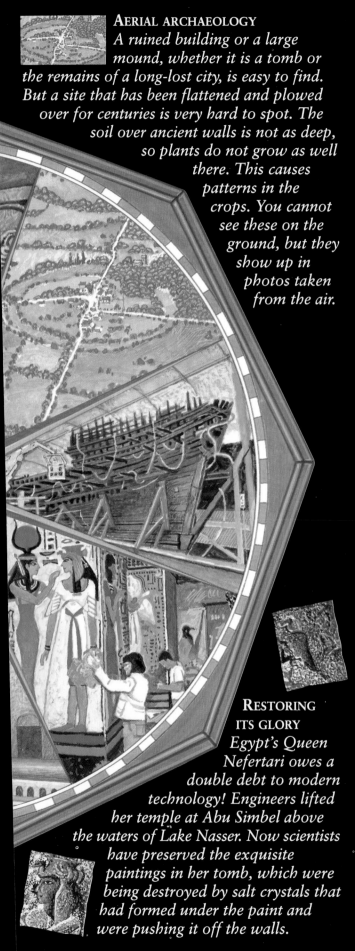

A ruined building or a large mound, whether it is a tomb or the remains of a long-lost city, is easy to find. But a site that has been flattened and plowed over for centuries is very hard to spot. The soil over ancient walls is not as deep, so plants do not grow as well there. This causes patterns in the crops. You cannot see these on the ground, but they show up in photos taken from the air.

RESTORING ITS GLORY

Egypt's Queen Nefertari owes a double debt to modern technology! Engineers lifted her temple at Abu Simbel above the waters of Lake Nasser. Now scientists have preserved the exquisite paintings in her tomb, which were being destroyed by salt crystals that had formed under the paint and were pushing it off the walls.

HAPPY FAMILIES

DNA is a substance in our body, inherited from both our parents. It determines how we look. Everyone's DNA is unique. Forensic scientists analyze DNA to identify criminals. Such analysis can tell archaeologists if bodies are related. It is now being used on Egyptian mummies.

Underwater magic

World War II (1939-1945) saw the development of the Aqua-lung, which allows divers to swim and use their arms freely. This led to the birth of marine archaeology. Dozens of shipwrecks have yielded up details of their cargoes and the secrets of their construction. Buildings drowned by the sea may also be excavated. Blocks from the lighthouse at Alexandria have been found recently, with statues that once adorned the city.

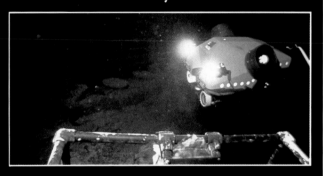

What next?

We have yet to identify Helen of Troy, Robin Hood remains hidden in the Greenwood, and Arthur is still the "once and future" king. There are lost people, treasures, cities, and civilizations to be found and new tools with which to find them. For archaeologists, the past has an exciting future. You can enjoy it, too.

TIME

c. 15,000 B.C. *Lascaux
cave paintings are made*

c. 3100-30 B.C. *Egypt flourishes*
c. 3000-1450 B.C. *Minoan civilization*

c. 2950-1500 B.C. *Stonehenge built, England*
c. 2600 B.C. *First Egyptian dam started*
c. 2500-1700 B.C. *Civilization in Indus Valley*
c. 2500-1500 B.C. *Bactrian culture at its peak*
c. 2000 B.C. *Hittites arrive in Anatolia (Turkey)*

c. 1900-1000 B.C. *Mycenaean civilization flourishes*
c. 1450 B.C. *Santorini volcano destroys Minoans*
c. 1367-1350 B.C. *Akhenaton rules Egypt*
c. 1190 B.C. *"Sea Peoples" defeat Hittites*
c. 1000 B.C.-A.D. *1500 Native American cultures
flourish in Ohio & Mississippi river valleys*

c. 800 B.C.-A.D. *100 Greek civilization*
c. 753 B.C.-A.D. *476 Roman civilization*
c. 612 B.C. *City of Babylon rebuilt*
c. 550 B.C.-A.D. *350 Meroe at its peak*
c. 432 B.C. *Statue of Zeus built at Olympia*
400s B.C.-A.D. *200s Petra is an important city*
c. 280 B.C. *Lighthouse at Alexandria built*
c. 272-231 B.C. *King Asoka rules India*
c. 221-210 B.C. *Cheng rules China*
c. 200 B.C.-A.D. *600 Nazca lines are created*
c. 83 B.C. *Sibylline prophesies are destroyed*
51-30 B.C. *Cleopatra* VII *rules Egypt*

A.D. *60-62 Queen Boudicca leads
English revolt against Romans*
66 B.C. *&* A.D. *132 Jewish
revolts against Roman rule*
A.D. *79 Town of Pompeii
destroyed by eruption
of Mount Vesuvius*

LINE

A.D. 270s Library of Alexandria is destroyed
A.D. 462 Statue of Zeus destroyed
A.D. 476 Roman Empire falls
c. A.D. 500 Rock Eagle Mound collapses
A.D. 600s King Arthur thought to exist
A.D. 600-1500 Easter Island statues erected
A.D. 800s Khmers build Angkor Wat & Thom

1336-1405 Timur Leng (Tamerlane) lives
1375 Lighthouse at Alexandria is destroyed
1521-1522 Tenochtitlan destroyed by the Spaniards
1545 The Mary Rose sinks off the English coast
1748-present Excavations at Pompeii & neighboring town of Herculaneum, Italy
1843 John Stephens finds Chichén Itzá
1870 Heinrich Schliemann finds Troy
1876 Schliemann excavates Mycenae
1893-1935 Arthur Evans finds Minoan remains
1911 Hiram Bingham finds Machu Picchu
1912 "Piltdown Man" bones discovered (but are proved to be a hoax in 1953)
1922 Howard Carter opens tomb of King Tutankhamen; Leonard Woolley excavates Ur
1940 Schoolboys find Lascaux cave paintings
1945-1948 Mortimer Wheeler excavates Indus Valley
1947 Dead Sea scrolls found in cave at Qumran
1974 Tomb of First Emperor discovered, China
1977 Tomb of Philip II of Macedonia discovered
1980s Examination of Chinese noblewoman
1991 Frozen man – "Ötzi" – discovered in glacier in Austrian mountains
1992 Minoan paintings discovered in ancient Egyptian tombs
1995 Tomb containing over 50 sons of King Rameses II discovered in Egypt
1996 Tomb of Queen Nefetari reopened

INDEX

Picture Credits *(t-top, m-middle, b-bottom, r-right, l-left)*: 4-5, 11 – Ancient Art & Architecture Collection; 13 – Bruce Coleman Collection; 17, 24, 29, 33, 34, 37 – Frank Spooner Pictures; 18 – York Archaeological Trust; 23 – Mary Evans Picture Library; 31 – James Davis Travel Photography.